Special thanks to Ted Wood for his help
with the editing of this translation.

Text copyright © 1992 by Tatsuharu Kodama
Text translation copyright © 1995 by Kazuko Hokumen-Jones
Illustrations copyright © 1995 by Noriyuki Ando

Text originally published in Japan by DOSHIN-SHA in 1992; this edition published in the United States of America in 1995 by Walker Publishing Company, Inc.

Published simultaneously in Canada by Thomas Allen & Son Canada, Limited, Markham, Ontario

Library of Congress Cataloging-in-Publication Data
Kodama, Tatsuharu, 1928–
[Shin-chan no sanrinsha. English]
Shin's tricycle / Tatsuharu Kodama ; illustrations by Noriyuki Ando ; English translation by Kazuko Hokumen-Jones.
p. cm.
ISBN 0-8027-8375-9. —ISBN 0-8027-8376-7 (reinforced)
1. Hiroshima-shi (Japan)—History—Bombardment, 1945—Personal narratives—Juvenile literature. 2. Atomic bomb victims—Japan—Hiroshima-shi—Biography—Juvenile literature. I. Ando, Noriyuki. II. Title.
D767.25.H6S51315 1995
940.54'26—dc20 95-7326
CIP
AC

Photographs on page 32 by Jin Yonenaga
Book design by Chin-Yee Lai

Printed in Hong Kong

2 4 6 8 10 9 7 5 3 1

Shin's Tricycle

Tatsuharu Kodama

Illustrations by **Noriyuki Ando**

English Translation by **Kazuko Hokumen-Jones**

Walker and Company

New York

Every August I am haunted by the same memory. In my mind I see my son, Shin, riding the red tricycle that he dreamed of getting for his birthday. But this happy picture disappears behind a cloud of smoke and ash. A darkness falls on my heart when I think of the one day in August that brought all our dreams to an end.

Fifty years ago, when Shin was three, our family lived in a small house near a quiet river that flowed through Hiroshima, Japan. Shin had two sisters, Michiko and Yoko. But his best friend was Kimi, the girl who lived next door. Each day they played house and looked at picture books, especially the one that showed the tricycle that Shin wanted so badly—even though he knew it was an impossible dream.

There weren't any tricycles anywhere in Japan! In 1941, Japan had attacked America and many other countries. And after four years of war, bicycles, temple bells, even pots and pans were melted down to build tanks and cannons. There were no new toys anywhere.

But Shin wanted a bike so much that one day he wouldn't eat anything. He pleaded to me, "Papa, you'll buy me a tricycle, won't you? Please, Papa, please!"

His mother lightly touched his shoulder and said, "We're sorry, Shin. You'll just have to learn to be patient. We all have to live without the things we want right now."

Shin was heartbroken, but he knew his mother was right.

Then, one day, Shin's uncle, a sailor in the Japanese navy, came to visit.

"Shin," he called. "Come here. I have something for you."

"What is it?" Shin asked with excitement, as he stared wide-eyed at the huge package in his uncle's arms.

"Take a guess," his uncle said. "It's something you *really, really* want."

With that, his uncle hid the gift behind him. Shin was so excited he jumped around him to reach the package. But his uncle, laughing all the while, kept the mystery gift hidden.

Just then, Shin saw a little red handle poking through the wrapping. "It's a tricycle!" Shin shrieked, not believing what he saw. But as he tore away the rest of the wrapping, his eyes filled with tears. "Oh, thank you, Uncle. Thank you so much. Where did you get it?"

"I found it hidden in the back of my closet," his uncle said. "I'm shipping out before your birthday so I wanted to give it to you now."

Quickly Shin jumped on the bike, and looking proudly at me, said, "Look, Papa, my dream came true."

The morning of August 6, 1945, was a beautiful one. The air was filled with the sandpapery sounds of cicadas rubbing their legs together in the nearby trees.

But the quiet of the morning was broken by another air-raid siren warning of an American bomb attack. When the siren stopped, Shin and Kimi ran to the backyard, giggling as they jumped on the tricycle and rode around the yard.

A group of soldiers, repairing the road in front of our house, laughed as they watched the red tricycle speed by with Shin and Kimi beaming like lanterns.

I too was laughing as I went back into our house to get ready for work. And then the unthinkable happened.

An explosion so terrible, a flash so blindingly bright, I thought the world had ended. Then, just as quickly, everything went black.

When I woke up, darkness surrounded me and I couldn't move. I was trapped—but where?

Then I saw a faint light coming through a small hole above me. I began to move my hands, carefully feeling the big wooden beams that were holding me down. I reached up and touched something smooth. It was the ceiling of our house! The whole house had collapsed on top of me.

Slowly I crawled toward the light and onto the roof. I stood looking into a hot, black wind. I couldn't believe my eyes. Nothing was left. No Kimi's house, no temple, no people, no Hiroshima.

I cried out into the wind, "Is anyone there?!"

"Help!" I heard Mother scream. "Help me, Nobuo!"

I stumbled over our fallen house and found Mother digging in the rubble. There was Shin, pinned under a big beam.

Quickly I lifted the beam while Mother gently pulled Shin out. His face was bleeding and swollen. He was too weak to talk but his hand still held the red handlebar grip from his tricycle. Kimi was gone, lost somewhere under the house.

Then I spotted the edges of two little dresses trapped beneath the roof. Behind them, a wall of fire raced toward our house.

"Michiko! Yoko!" I screamed. "I'm coming!"

With all my strength, I tried to lift the roof beams, but couldn't. The fire was very close now, and it was so hot I feared my clothes would start burning. Suddenly, the beam on top of Michiko and Yoko burst into flames.

"Michiko! Yoko!" I cried in horror. I was helpless to save my girls. There was nothing I could do. But Shin still had a chance, so Mother and I rushed him away from the raging fire to the river.

The survivors all gathered on the riverbank. It was a horrible sight. Everyone was burned, and they were crying, moaning, screaming for water.

"Water. I want water," pleaded Shin in a faint voice. I wanted to help him so much. But all around, people were dying when they drank the water, so I didn't dare give him any.

"Papa," Shin whispered so quietly I could barely hear him. "My . . . my . . . tricy—"

I squeezed his hand that still held the plastic grip. "Shin," I said, "You still have the handle in your hand."

His swollen face seemed to brighten, and a little smile peeked through. But that night he died, ten days before his fourth birthday.

The next day, I went back to our house. There I found the little bones of Michiko and Yoko lying together. I burst into tears. "I'm sorry, my loves. Please forgive me."

After I buried them, I cried for a long time, remembering how happy they had been just the day before.

The next evening I dug a grave in our backyard for Shin. But before I buried him, Kimi's mother arrived carrying Kimi's body. "They were such good friends," she said sadly. "We should bury them together, Nobuo."

So, Kimi and Shin were buried together holding hands, along with Shin's treasured tricycle, which we had found in the rubble.

Every evening after that we stood by the river and cried out our children's names. "Shin! Michiko! Yoko!"

Forty years passed after the atomic bomb turned Hiroshima into a desert, and there was new life all around the city. People had worried that nothing would ever grow again, but trees and grass sprouted everywhere. Children laughed and played in the parks.

I remembered the smiles of my own children, and my heart still ached with the memory.

For many years Mother and I had been comforted by knowing our children were so close by. But we had always intended to give the children a proper burial in a cemetery. One day we decided the time had come to move them. We began digging in the backyard, and Kimi's mother joined us.

After a few minutes of digging, I hit something metal. I looked closely and saw a rusty pipe sticking through the dirt.

"Look, Mother, it's the tricycle! I had forgotten it was here."

Before I knew it, I was crying. I had to turn away. I just couldn't look at it.

"Look, Papa, there's something white," Mother said.

We all stared at the little white bones of Kimi and Shin, hand in hand as we had placed them.

Wars are always brutal. No matter who starts one, innocent people die—even children like Shin.

With tears in my eyes, I gently lifted Shin's tricycle.

"This should never again happen to children," I said. "Maybe if enough people could see Shin's tricycle, they would remember that the world should be a peaceful place where children can play and laugh."

The next day I took the tricycle to the Peace Museum in Hiroshima. Now Shin's story helps keep the dream of peace alive for children around the world.

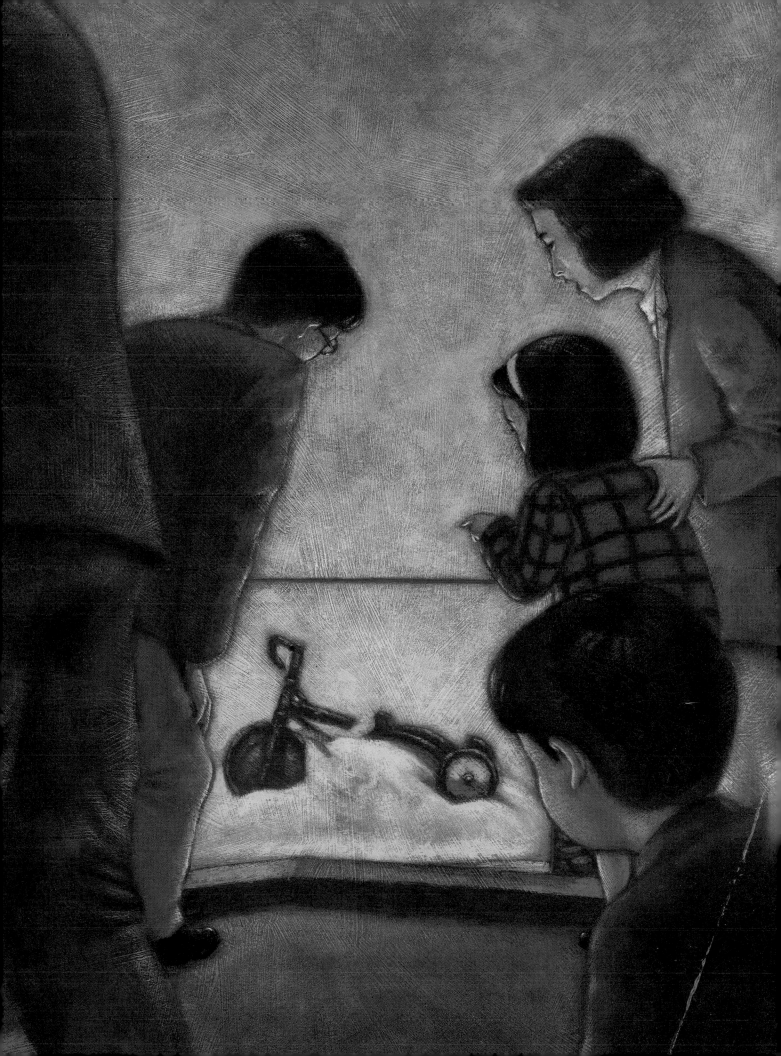

Author's Note

Sadly, the story told in *Shin's Tricycle* is true. Shin Tetsutani was killed when the atomic bomb was dropped on Hiroshima less than two weeks before his fourth birthday. Although his life was short, it had a great purpose. Each year 1.5 million people visit the Peace Museum and see the exhibit about Shin's life. His battered tricycle serves as a reminder of all the young victims of that tragic day—and as a symbol of the joyful and innocent time that childhood should be. Shin inspires us all to strive for a lasting peace, so that the events of that terrible day, August 6, 1945, are never repeated.

Shin, age three, with his sister Michiko, age six.

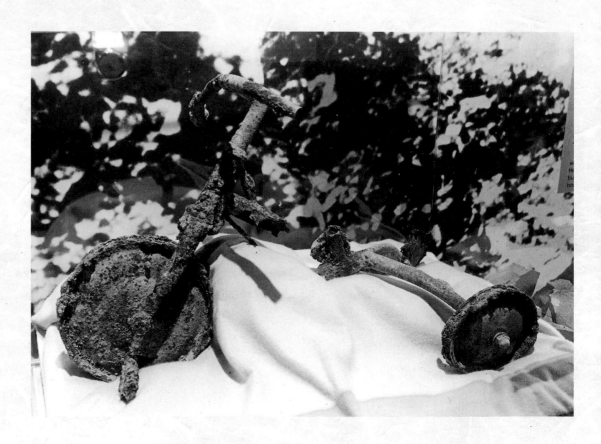

Shin's tricycle on display at the Peace Museum.